T... **5**

Friends ... *ed by your cards.
They'll love* ... *them so much they'll keep and
frame every one for their homes.*

Celena - Pale Green paper • Cardstock (White, Dark Green, Medium Green, Celery Green) • Photocopies • Fiskars Deckle scissors • Double-stick tape
Make Tea-Bag Folds following instructions on page 18. Pin-Punch letters using alphabet on page 7 and border using pattern on page 27. Cut out leaves and stems using patterns on page 27, Pin-Punch edges. Assemble page.

Oriental Card - Design Originals Asian Lady Tea-Bag paper • 4½" x 6" Ivory card • 5½" x 8½" Ivory paper for liner • Sulky Iris thread • Paula Hallinan Brass flower corner stencil • Stylus • Double-stick tape
Pierce holes and Embroider teardrop using pattern on page 23. Make Tea-Bag Folds following instructions on page 18. Emboss card corners following instructions on page 6. Assemble card.

Embroidery on Paper

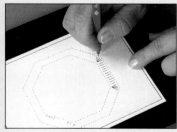 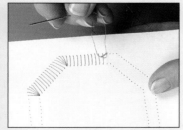 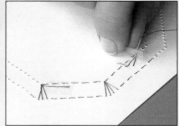 

1. Position pattern on the **FRONT** of cardstock. Tape in place. Place cardstock on top of craft foam. **2.** Holding tool vertically, use a needle tool to pierce holes. **3.** Remove pattern. **Tip -** If you are using heavy thread or ribbon, you may need to make holes larger. Run the head of a large embroidery needle through holes you have already pierced.

4. Thread a needle with floss. Bring the needle up at the odd numbered holes and go down at the even number holes.
Tip - When a pattern indicates 1 to 7 spacing, come up at 1, count to the 7th hole, go down in the 7th hole, up in next hole to the right, down in the hole next to 1, up in 3rd hole, etc. Always count hole 1 as the first hole and double-check to make

sure you have the correct number of holes.
Tip - Always try to have short stitches on the back and long stitches on the front especially on circles. Keep stitches away from edges of card.
5. Use a small piece of clear tape next to holes to secure thread on back of cardstock.
6. Finish the card as desired.
Tip - Beads can be added while

you are stitching.
Anchoring Tip - When required to come back up in the same hole that was just completed, wrap thread around a previous stitch on back then come back up through hole.
Triangle Shapes Tip - No matter how many holes are on the side of a triangle, the 2 hole is always the second hole from the top on the opposite side.

Girl Card - 4½" x 6" White card • 5½" x 8½" White paper for liner and 4 squares for tea-bag folds • Photocopies • Sulky Pink and Green thread • UIT Holland Brass flower stencil • Stylus • Double-stick tape
Pierce holes and Embroider diamond in a square using pattern on page 10. Make Tea-Bag Folds following instructions on page 18. Emboss card following instructions on page 6. Assemble card.

These cards and memory pages combine three different techniques to give you even more crafting fun!

Flutter-Bys - Design Originals Butterflies on Blue paper • Cardstock (White, Purple, Yellow) • Photocopies • 3¾" Purple butterfly • Sulky Purple & Yellow thread • Fiskars Celestial Corner scissors • Double-stick tape
Pierce holes and Embroider butterfly using pattern on page 11. Pin-Punch letters using alphabet on page 7.
Cut out Purple butterfly shape using pattern.
Pin-Punch edges of butterfly.
Make Tea-Bag Folds using instructions on page 18.
Assemble page.

Shoe Card - Design Originals Antique Shoes paper • 4½" x 6" Cream card • 5½" x 8½" Cream paper for liner Sulky Peach and Rust thread • UIT Holland Brass border stencil • Stylus • Double-stick tape
Pierce holes and Embroider frame using pattern on page 23. Make Tea-Bag Folds following instructions on page 18. Emboss card following instructions on page 6. Assemble card.

Garden Gate Card - Design Originals Seasonal Postcards paper • 4½" x 6" Light Gold card • 5½" x 8½" Ivory paper for liner • Sulky Variegated Gold thread • Linda ♥ design Brass flower corner & UIT Holland border stencils • Stylus • Double-stick tape
Pierce holes and Embroider Garden Gate using pattern on page 10. Make Tea-Bag Folds following instructions on page 18. Emboss card following instructions on page 6. Assemble card.

Pin-Punch & Embroidery with Picture Tea-Bag Folds

Pin-Punch and Embroider colorful accents for your cards and album pages. Add Tea-Bag Folds to make them true works of art.

Butterfly Card - Design Originals Feng Shui Tea-Bag paper • 4½" x 6" Ivory card • 5½" x 8½" Ivory paper for liner • Sulky Light Green thread • Linda ♡ design Brass border stencil • Stylus • Double-stick tape
Pierce holes and Embroider butterfly using pattern on page 11. Make Tea-Bag Folds following instructions on page 18. Emboss card following instructions on page 6. Assemble card.

Baby Boy - Sonburn Daisies & Dots paper • Cardstock (Yellow, Bright Yellow, White, Wedgewood Blue • Sulky Royal Blue thread • Photocopies • Heart templates • Fiskars scissors (Deckle, Clouds, Blossom Corner) • Double-stick tape
Pierce holes and Embroider heart using pattern on page 14. Pin-Punch letters using alphabet on page 7 and border using pattern on page 27. Make Tea-Bag Folds following instruction on page 18. Assemble page.

Cross Card - 4½" x 6" White card • 5½" x 8½" White paper for liner • Sulky Metallic Variegated thread • Lasting Impressions Brass flower corner stencil • Stylus • Sandylion iris sticker • Double-stick tape
Pierce holes and Embroider cross using pattern on page 11. Emboss card following instructions on page 6. Assemble card.

Heart Card - Design Originals Seasonal Postcards paper • 4½" x 6" White card • 5½" x 8½" White paper for liner • Sulky Light Red thread • Brass dove & Lasting Impressions double heart stencils • Stylus • Double-stick tape
Pierce holes and Embroider heart using pattern on page 14. Make Tea-Bag Folds following instructions on page 18. Emboss card following instructions on page 6. Assemble card.

Love Swans

Embroider graceful swans to enhance the front of a greeting card or the title strip on an album page.

Swan Card - 4½" x 6" White card • 5½" x 8½" White paper for liner • Sulky Purple thread • Printworks flower stickers • Double-stick tape
Pierce holes and Embroider swan. Assemble card.

1. To emboss, use a light box, stylus, a brass stencil and a card or cardstock.

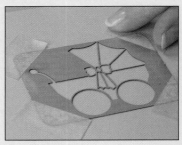

2. After the card has been pierced (see page 2), position stencil on the front of the card. Tape in place .

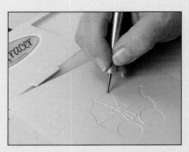

3. Open card, turn it over, place on light box with stencil underneath. Outline edges of design with a stylus.

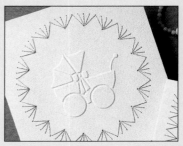

4. Remove stencil and fold card with raised design on the outside.
5. Now you are ready to embroider the design.

Love - Design Original Water & Swirls paper • Ivory and Dark Teal cardstock • Sulky Variegated Teal thread • Fiskars Summit Corner and Corkscrew scissors • Double-stick tape
Pierce holes and Embroider swans. Pin-Punch letters using alphabet on page 7. Assemble page.

Pin-Punch Alphabet

Make a photocopy of the alphabet on vellum. Make a pencil line on the **BACK** of paper to be Pin-Punched, align each letter on the line (on the back of paper) and Pin-Punch. Place the next letter adjacent to the previous letter and Pin-Punch, continue writing the phrase.

If you want the lettering smaller, reduce the alphabet when photocopying. Keep vellum for future lettering projects.

Embroidery

Pierce designs for embroidery from the **FRONT** of paper.

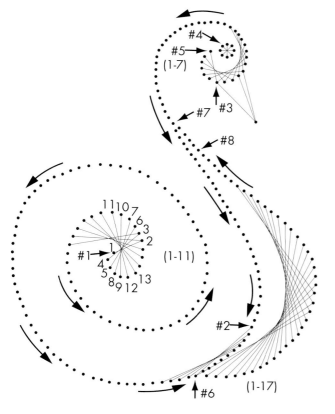

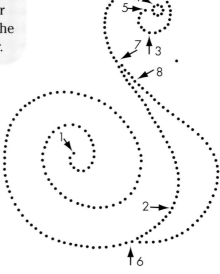

Swans - Start at #1 and stitch 1 to 11 spacing to #2. Anchor thread. At #3 make 3 long stitches for beak. At #4 stitch eye. Start at #5 and stitch 1 to 7 spacing to #6 and anchor thread. Start at #6 and stitch 1 to 17 spacing to #7. At #8 come up, go over all threads and go through #8. Anchor thread.

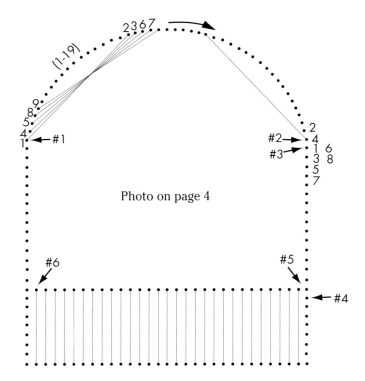

Garden Gate - Start at #1, stitch 1 to 19 spacing, stopping at #2. At #3, begin border stitch to #4. From #5, make vertical stitches across bottom. At #6, border stitch back across to #4 and continue border stitch completely around pattern ending at #3.

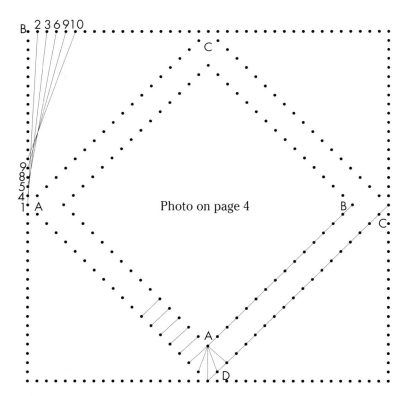

Diamond in a Square - Stitch short straight stitches around diamond. Outline diamond with long stitches from A to B and C to D. Repeat around diamond. For frame, make triangle corner. Start at A, down at 2, up at 3, down at 4, continue to C. Anchor and come up at C. Do remaining corners. Outline each corner with 2 long stitches; A to B, B to C.

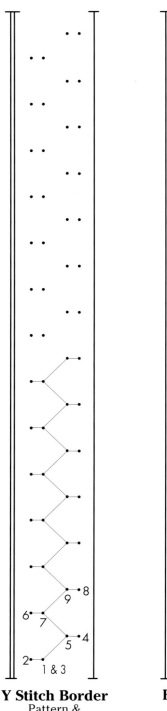

Y Stitch Border
Pattern &
Stitch Diagram

Photo on page 16

Border Stitch
Diagram
Use bead or
make French
Knot at center

Photo on page 17

Embroidery
Pierce designs for
embroidery from the
FRONT of paper.

Photo on page 33

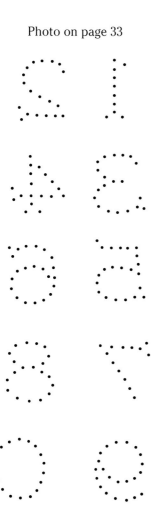

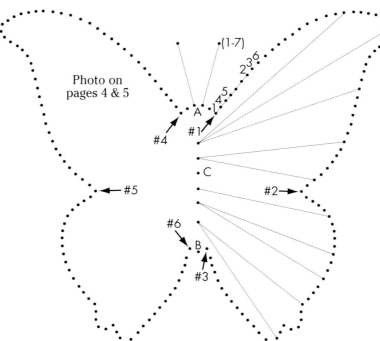

Photo on pages 4 & 5

Butterfly - Start at #1 and stitch 1 to 7 spacing to #2, anchor thread. At #2, stitch 1 to 7 spacing to #3, anchor thread. Start at A and border stitch top holes and make 2 long stitches. Make French knot at top of long stitches. At #4 , stitch 1 to 7 spacing to #5, anchor thread. At #5, stitch 1 to 7 spacing to #6. Make 2 border stitches at B. Make long stitches inside wings if desired.

Pin-Punch Numbers

Make a photocopy of numbers on vellum. Make a pencil line on **BACK** of paper to be Pin-Punched, align each number on the line (on the back of paper) and Pin-Punch. Place the next number adjacent to the previous letter and Pin-Punch, continue writing the phrase.

If you want the numbers smaller, reduce the numbers when photocopying. Keep the vellum for future numbering of projects.

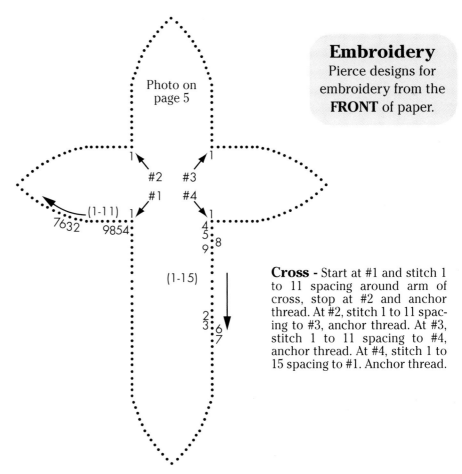

Photo on page 5

Embroidery

Pierce designs for embroidery from the **FRONT** of paper.

Cross - Start at #1 and stitch 1 to 11 spacing around arm of cross, stop at #2 and anchor thread. At #2, stitch 1 to 11 spacing to #3, anchor thread. At #3, stitch 1 to 11 spacing to #4, anchor thread. At #4, stitch 1 to 15 spacing to #1. Anchor thread.

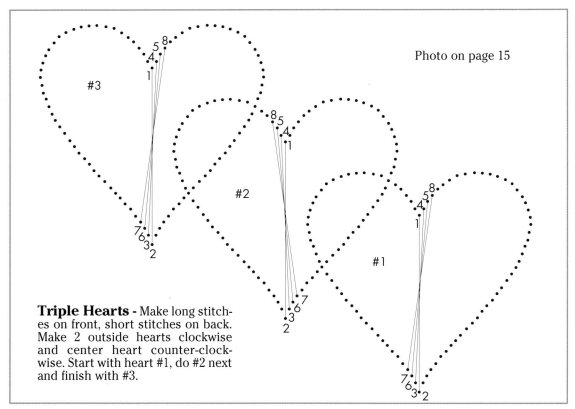

Photo on page 15

Triple Hearts - Make long stitches on front, short stitches on back. Make 2 outside hearts clockwise and center heart counter-clockwise. Start with heart #1, do #2 next and finish with #3.

Embroidery
Pierce designs for embroidery from the **FRONT** of paper.

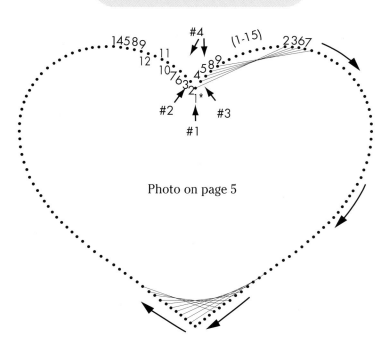

(1-15)

#4

#2   #3

#1

Photo on page 5

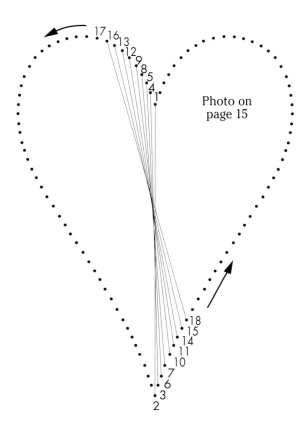

Photo on page 15

Wide Heart - Start at #1 and stitch 1 to 15 spacing. Continue around heart back to #1. Anchor threads. #2 & #3 are fill-in areas. Up at *, down at 2, up at 3 through 12. At #4 (4th hole) come up, go around thread & back down at #4. Repeat on other side.

Large Heart - Make long stitches on front, short stitches on back around heart. Stitch either clockwise or counter-clockwise.

'I Love You' Hearts

Hearts, hearts, hearts… adorn cards and pages filled with love! Use them for Valentines or just to say 'I Love You'.

Long Heart Card - 4½" x 6" Ivory card • 8½" x 5½" Ivory paper for liner • DMC Metallic Purple embroidery floss • Fiskars Nostalgia scissors • American Traditional Iris Brass stencil • Stylus • Double-stick tape
Pierce holes and Embroider heart with 2 strands of floss. Emboss right bottom corner with iris following instructions on page 6. Assemble card.

These Pin-Punch and Embroidery pieces say it all!

Friendship - Karen Foster Designs Red plaid paper • White and Deep Red cardstock • Sulky Red thread • Heart templates • Fiskars scissors (Colonial, Deckle, Regal Corner) • Double-stick tape
Pierce holes and Embroider hearts. Pin-Punch letters using alphabet on page 7. Assemble page.

Triple Heart Card - 4½" x 6" Ivory card • 8½" x 5½" Ivory paper for liner • Sulky Variegated Teal thread • Linda ♡ design flower corner Brass stencils • Stylus • Double-stick tape
Pierce holes and Embroider the hearts. Emboss the opposite corners of card following instruction on page 6. Assemble card.

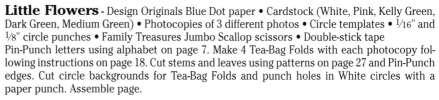

Green Bird Card - Design Originals Seasonal Postcards paper • 4¼" x 5½" Dark Green card • 5" x 7¾" White paper for liner • 3" square of Pale Green cardstock • Kreinik Metallic Gold ombre thread • Metallic Gold paint pen • Double-stick tape
Pierce holes and Embroider border using pattern on page 10. Make Tea-Bag Folds following instructions on page 18. Place folds on 3" square and trim leaving ⅛" border. Assemble card.

Little Flowers - Design Originals Blue Dot paper • Cardstock (White, Pink, Kelly Green, Dark Green, Medium Green) • Photocopies of 3 different photos • Circle templates • ¹⁄₁₆" and ⅛" circle punches • Family Treasures Jumbo Scallop scissors • Double-stick tape
Pin-Punch letters using alphabet on page 7. Make 4 Tea-Bag Folds with each photocopy following instructions on page 18. Cut stems and leaves using patterns on page 27 and Pin-Punch edges. Cut circle backgrounds for Tea-Bag Folds and punch holes in White circles with a paper punch. Assemble page.

Purple Pansy Card - Design Originals Purple Pansies Tea-Bag paper • 4½" x 5" Purple • ⅜" x 4¼" and 1" x 5½" strips of Lavender suede paper • ⅛" Rainbow ribbon • Double-stick tape
Pierce holes and Embroider border using pattern on page 30. Make Tea-Bag Folds following instructions on page 18. Assemble card.

Grape Card - Design Originals Grapes Tea-Bag paper • 4¼" x 5½" Lavender card • 5" x 7¾" White paper for liner • 1" strip of Purple suede paper for edge of card • Kreinik Lavender & Green braid • Yellow beading thread • Beading needle • Yellow seed beads • Fiskars Leaf & Deckle scissors • Double-stick tape
Pierce holes and Embroider border using pattern on page 30. Tape end of Yellow thread inside, bring to front and add beads along pattern. To add a bead, come up from back, place bead on thread and go back through same hole. Make Tea-Bag Folds following instructions on page 18. Trim edge of card with Leaf scissors. Tape suede paper behind edge and trim with Deckle scissors. Assemble card.

'Mother' - Design Originals Wallpaper on Sepia paper • Cream & Terra Cotta cardstock • DMC Brown craft thread • Brown beading thread • Beading needle • Copper seed beads • Templates (circle, oval, rectangle) • Fiskars scissors (Nostalgia Corner, Majestic, Deckle) • Double-stick tape
Pin–Punch letters using alphabet on page 7. Pierce holes and Embroider border using pattern on page10. Tape end of Brown thread inside, bring to front and add beads along pattern. To add a bead, come up from back, place bead on thread and go back through same hole. Assemble page.

Stitch Cards

Stitching with decorative threads brings glitter and glitz to simple cards and album pages.

MATERIALS: 4¼" x 5½" card • Paper for liners • Assorted threads • Beads • Silk embroidery (chenille) needles • Single point needle tool • Craft foam • Scissors • Magic transparent tape • Double-stick tape • (Optional: Sewing wax)

INSTRUCTIONS:

1. Place the FRONT of card on craft foam, place pattern on fold or edge. If placing pattern at inside fold, place a single line along the fold. If placing pattern on the outside edge, place a double line along edge.

2. Tape pattern in place. Pierce dots with a needle tool. Remove tape and pattern.

3. Tape thread at hole #1 inside the card (to secure it without a knot). Bring thread up at #1 and stitch pattern. When complete, tape thread on the inside to secure it.

4. Adhere a paper liner over the inside stitching.

5. Embellish the front of the card with Tea-Bag Folds, cardstock and decorative papers.

Stitch with decorative threads to create cards and album pages with a touch of class.

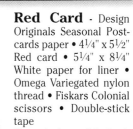

Red Card - Design Originals Seasonal Postcards paper • 4¼" x 5½" Red card • 5¼" x 8¼" White paper for liner • Omega Variegated nylon thread • Fiskars Colonial scissors • Double-stick tape
Pierce holes and Embroider border using pattern on page 10. Make Tea-Bag Folds following instructions on page 18. Insert liner and trim 2 edges of card and liner with Colonial scissors. Assemble card.

Brown Card - Design Originals Seasonal Postcards paper • 4¼" x 5½" Light Green card • 3" x 4¾" and 1" x 5½" strip of Rust suede paper • Caron Parfait Water thread • Fiskars Art Deco scissors • Double-stick tape
Pierce holes and Embroider border using pattern on page 26. Make Tea-Bag Folds following instructions on page 18. Assemble card.

Flower Card - Design Originals Flowers Tea-Bag paper • 4¼" x 5½" Dark Green card • 5" x 7¾" White paper for liner • Kreinik Metallic Copper braid • Fiskars scissors (Nostalgia Corner, Corkscrew) • Metallic Copper paint pen • Double-stick tape
Pierce holes and Embroider border using pattern on page 26. Make Tea-Bag Folds following instructions on page 18. Trim edge and corners and outline edge with pen. Assemble card.

Picture Tea-Bag Folds

1. Photocopy photos or designs (or scan & print with a computer). Use lightweight paper for easier folding. Cut 1³/₄" or 2" squares out of plastic for a cutting template.

2. Center template on picture, make several pencil marks on template at appropriate areas of picture so you can place pieces in the exact same position on the next piece of paper. It is possible to use only 4 photocopies. Cut 4 squares of the face for the 4 center folds. Cut 4 more squares from another area for the back 4 folds.

3. When folding a picture diamond, fold 4 different squares. Each square will show a quarter section of the center of the picture... you will have a pointed end with a different portion of the picture. Choose which pointed end you prefer for the background squares and make 4 identical squares.

4. Using 4 picture squares, place one diamond on a small piece of transparent tape. Continue adding the diamonds to complete the picture.

5. Tape remaining diamonds together and add tape under the picture diamonds, rotating to fill the spaces between pointed ends.

NOTE: When folding the 4 picture diamonds, fold 4 squares up to Step 3. You can then see how to proceed with Step 4 to obtain different quarters of the picture. The square is rotated ¹/₄ turn with each fold.

Make 8 Diamonds

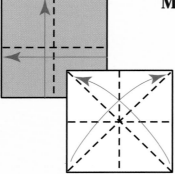

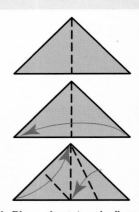

1. With the pattern side up, fold the square side to side in both directions.
2. Turn pattern down and fold at an angle in both directions.

3. Pinch the outside tips of triangle base, push to center and fold with 2 points at each end of triangle base.

4. Place the triangle flat with the base toward you. Fold top right point over to the left, making 3 points on left. Fold right point down to center. Fold left point up to center.

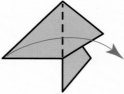
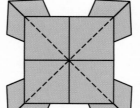

5. Fold the triangle just formed to the right.

6. Fold the upper left point to the right.

7. Fold left point down to center. Fold top right point up to center.

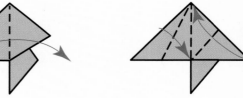
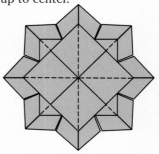

8. Fold the triangle just formed to the left.

9. Place 4 pieces in a square.

10. Arrange 4 more pieces on top of the first square.

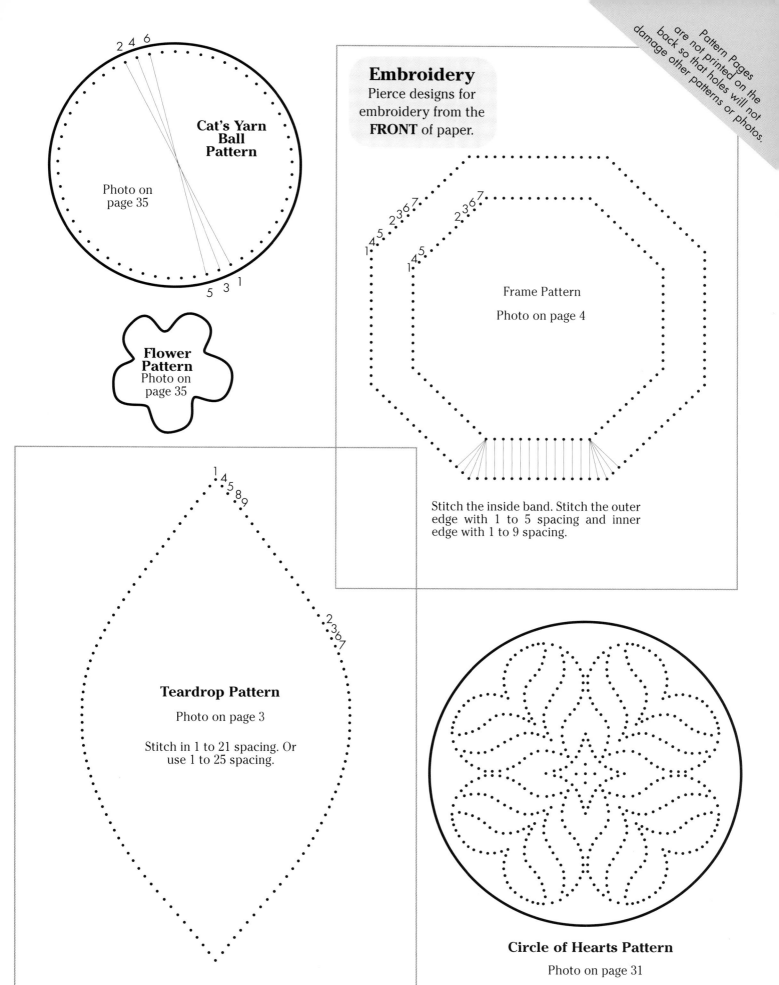

Cat's Yarn Ball Pattern

Photo on page 35

Embroidery
Pierce designs for embroidery from the **FRONT** of paper.

Frame Pattern
Photo on page 4

Stitch the inside band. Stitch the outer edge with 1 to 5 spacing and inner edge with 1 to 9 spacing.

Flower Pattern
Photo on page 35

Teardrop Pattern

Photo on page 3

Stitch in 1 to 21 spacing. Or use 1 to 25 spacing.

Circle of Hearts Pattern

Photo on page 31

Hearts & Ribbon Pattern

Photo on page 32

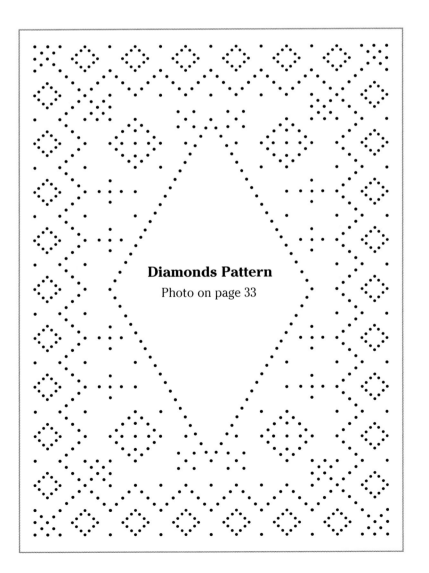

Diamonds Pattern

Photo on page 33

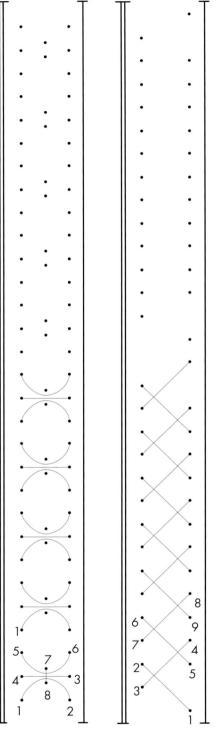

Border Pattern

Photo on
page 17

Come up at 7, pull 3
strands to center
and go down at 8.

**Criss-Cross
Border Pattern**

Photo on
page 17

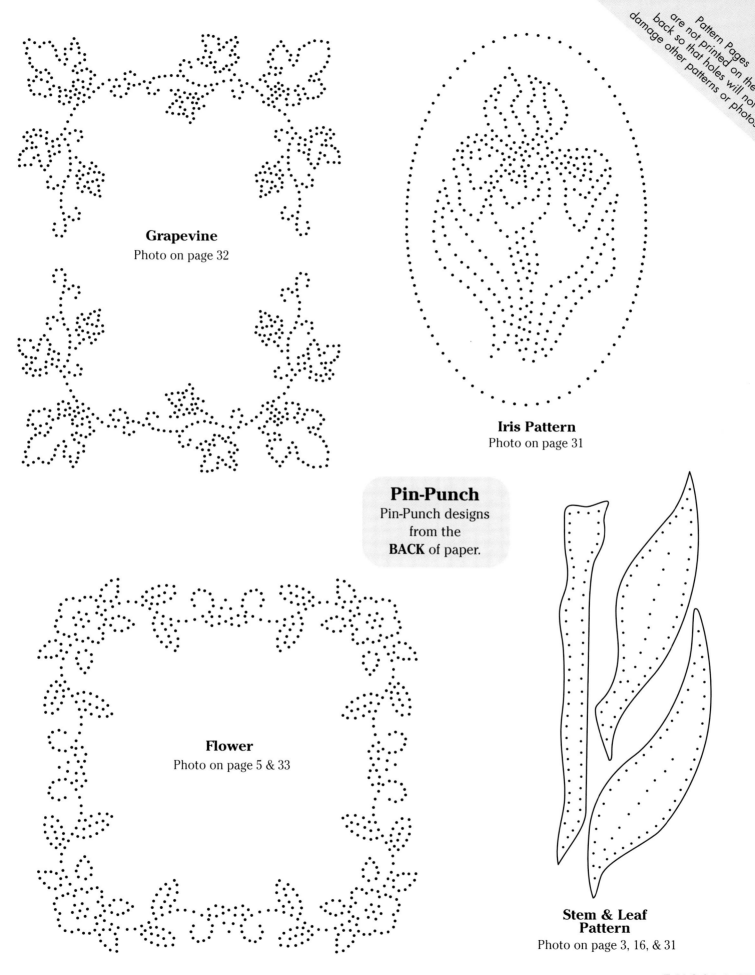

Grapevine
Photo on page 32

Iris Pattern
Photo on page 31

Pin-Punch
Pin-Punch designs
from the
BACK of paper.

Flower
Photo on page 5 & 33

**Stem & Leaf
Pattern**
Photo on page 3, 16, & 31

Pin-Punch
Pin-Punch designs from the **BACK** of paper.

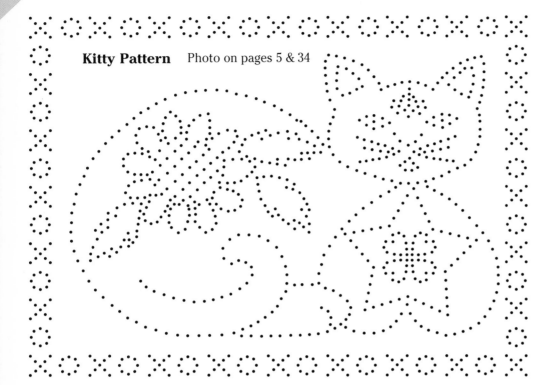

Kitty Pattern   Photo on pages 5 & 34

Rose & Hearts Pattern

Photo on pages 32 & 34

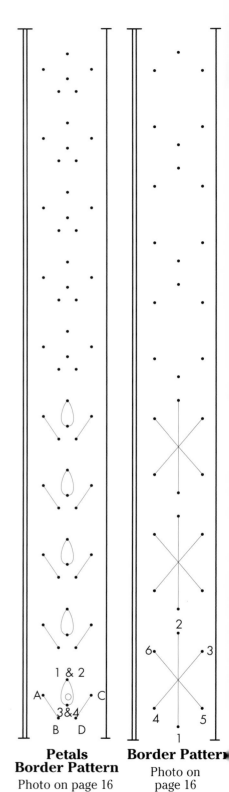

Petals Border Pattern

Photo on page 16

Border Pattern▶

Photo on page 16

Petals - For petals, come up at 1, leave loop and go down through same hole. Go up at 3 and down at 4 catching loop. A to B and C to D are done with second color. Add beads with matching thread.

Beads add a special bit of glamour to simple designs. On white backgrounds, beads gleam and glow.

Blooming Girl Card - 4½" x 6" Blue card • Green and 4" x 4¾" White cardstock • Pink paper for tea-bag folds • Photocopies • Fiskars Deckle scissors • Double-stick tape
Pin-Punch border using pattern on page 26. Make 4 Pink and 4 photocopy Tea-Bag Folds following instructions on page 18. Cut leaves and stem using pattern on page 27. Pin-Punch edges. Assemble card.

Spring Day - Design Originals paper (Pink Ticking Stripe, Pink Dot, Cherry Blossoms Tea-Bag) • Pink cardstock • 2 Lavender 1⅝" butterfly die cuts • Tulip die cuts (Yellow, Lavender, Hot Pink) • Fiskars Corkscrew scissors • Double-stick tape
Pin-Punch letters using alphabet on page 7 and edges of die cuts. Make Tea-Bag Folds following instructions on page 18. Assemble page.

Iris Card - 4¼" x 5½" White card • 3" x 4½" White cardstock • 3¼" x 5" Purple suede paper • Purple seed beads • White beading thread • Beading needle • Avec B.V. Brass corner stencil • Stylus • Oval template• Fiskars Deckle scissors • Double-stick tape
Pin-Punch iris using pattern on page 27. Sew beads around border. Emboss corners following instructions on page 6. Assemble card.

Circle of Hearts Card - 5½" square White card • 3½" White cardstock and 5" Red suede paper squares • Red and White seed beads • White beading thread • Beading needle • Avec B.V. Brass swirl border stencil • Stylus • Circle templates • Fiskars Corner Rounder • Double-stick tape
Pin-Punch circle of hearts using pattern on page 23. Sew beads around hearts. Emboss border following instructions on page 6. Assemble card.

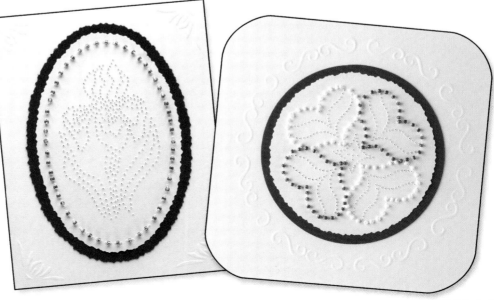

Hearts & Ribbon Card - Design Originals Seasonal Postcards paper • 4¼" x 5½" Red card • 3⅝" x 5⅛" Yellow and 3½" x 5" White cardstock • Fiskars Regal Corner & Celestial Corner scissors • Double-stick tape
Pin-Punch border using pattern on page 26. Assemble card.

New Baby Girl - Design Originals Little Baby Faces paper • Pale Pink & Celery Green cardstock • Computer printed journaling on White paper • Heart & oval templates • Corner Rounder punch • Fiskars Cloud & Stamp scissors
Pin-Punch heart border and hearts using rose pattern on page 30 and letters using alphabet on page 7. Assemble page.

Wedding Day - Design Originals Music Melody paper • Cardstock (Black, Deep Red, White) • Computer printed verse on White paper • Circle template • Fiskars Deckle and Nostalgia Corner scissors
Pin-Punch letters using alphabet on page 7. Assemble page.

Grapevine Card -
Design Originals Seasonal Postcards paper • 5" x 6½" White card • 4½" x 6" Pink moire paper • 4" x 5½" White cardstock • Fiskars Corner Rounder • Fiskars Nostalgia Corner scissors • Double-stick tape
Pin-Punch border using pattern on page 27. Make Tea-Bag Folds following instructions on page 18. Assemble card.

Gabrielle Christina
July 2, 2000
8:42 pm
8 pounds 4 ¾ ounces
20 inches long

Great Pin-Punch Projects

Pin-Punch frames to add textural and visual interest to your paper projects. Never have techniques been so easy with such spectacular results.

Summer Camp - 2 sheets of Design Originals Deep Blue Sea paper • Lime Green and Deep Red cardstock • Fiskars Elegance and Rounder Corner scissors
Pin-Punch letters and numbers using alphabet on page 7. Cut fish and bubbles from the second piece of paper. Assemble page.

Use these fabulous design ideas for your memory pages and cards or mix and match the full size patterns to make your own beautiful creations!

Diamonds Card - Design Originals Travel Postcards paper • 5" x 7" White card • 4½" x 6½" Blue handmade paper • 4¼" x 5¾" White cardstock • Fiskars Deckle scissors • Double-stick tape
Pin-Punch diamonds using pattern on page 26. Make Tea-Bag Folds following instructions on page 18. Assemble card.

Flower Border Card - Design Originals Seasonal Postcards paper • 5½" square Terra Cotta card • 4½" square White cardstock • Fiskars Regal Corner scissors • Double-stick tape
Pin-Punch border using pattern on page 27. Make Tea-Bag Folds following instructions on page 18. Assemble card.

Embossed, Stitched, Pin-Punched and Tea-bag Fold projects are fun and easy. Even your friends who say, "Crafts aren't my thing", will enjoy these fabulous ideas. All you need to do is gather your supplies and get started today!.

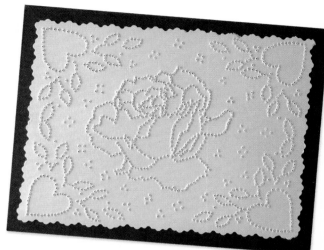

Kitty - 4¼" x 5¾" Design Originals Petals paper • 4½" x 6" Purple card • 3¾" x 4¾" White cardstock • 4¼" x 5½" White paper for liner • Fiskars Deckle and Blossom Corner scissors • Double-stick tape
Pin-Punch cat using pattern on page 30. Assemble card.

Rose - 4½" x 6" Dark Green card • 4¼" x 5½" White paper for liner • 3½" x 4¾" Cream cardstock • Fiskars Ripple scissors • Double-stick tape
Pin-Punch rose using pattern on page 30. Assemble card.

Hearts & Flowers - Design Originals Sunflowers Tea-Bag paper • 4½" x 6" Green card • 3½" x 4¾" White cardstock • 4¼" x 5½" White paper for liner • Fiskars Nostalgia Corner scissors • Double-stick tape
Pin-Punch corners using rose pattern on page 30. Make Tea-Bag Folds following instructions on page 18. Assemble card.

Mommy & Me - Design Originals Travel Postcard paper • Cardstock (Forest Green, Rust, Ivory) • Fiskars Deckle & Blossom Corner scissors
Pin-Punch hearts using rose pattern page 30 and letters using alphabet on page 7. Assemble page.